Creative Spaces
A Daily Planner with Notepad

Activinotes

Activinotes

DAILY JOURNALS, PLANNERS, NOTEBOOKS AND OTHER BLANK BOOKS

A Daily Planner

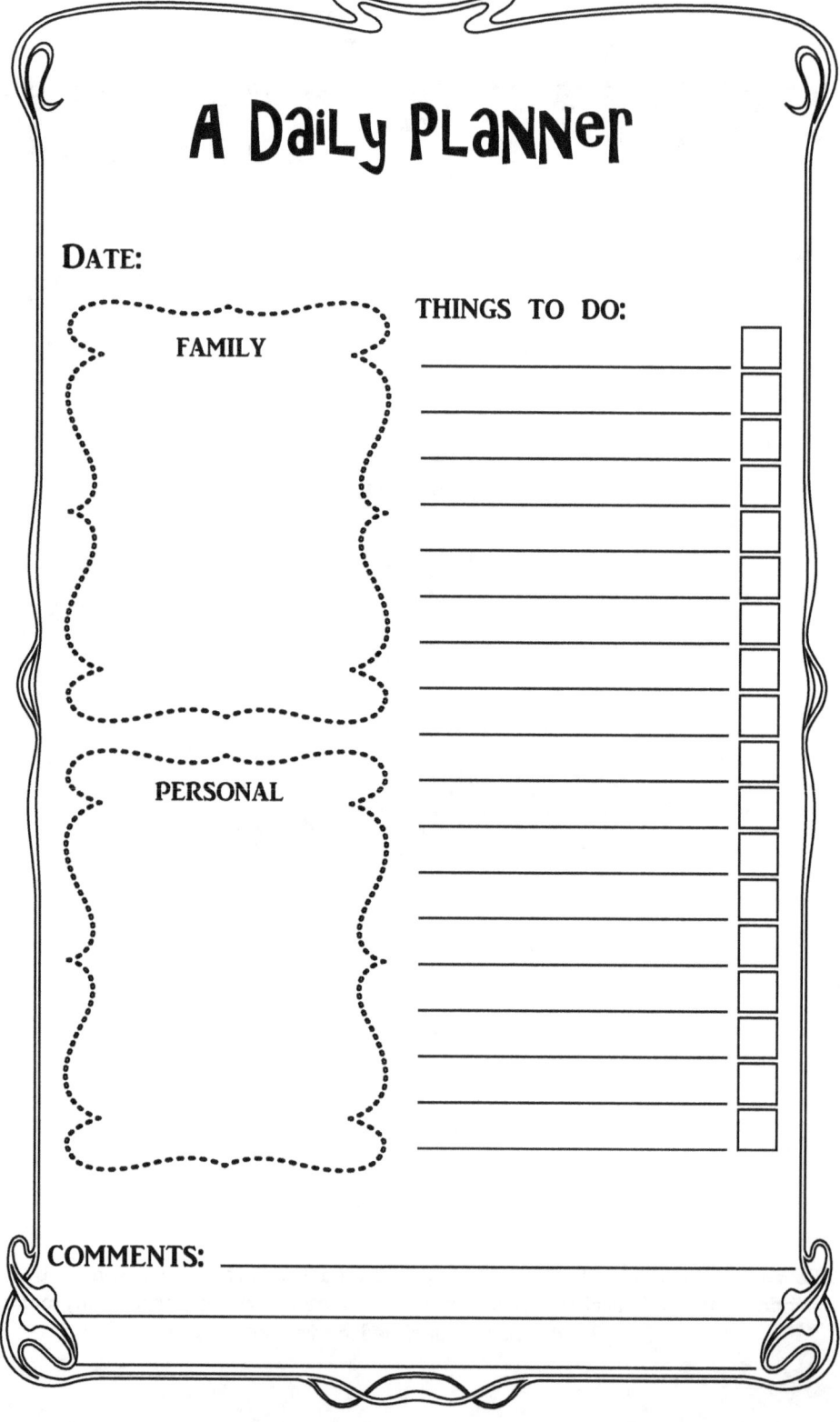

DATE:

FAMILY

PERSONAL

THINGS TO DO:

COMMENTS:

A Daily Planner

DATE:

FAMILY

PERSONAL

THINGS TO DO:
_____ ☐
_____ ☐
_____ ☐
_____ ☐
_____ ☐
_____ ☐
_____ ☐
_____ ☐
_____ ☐
_____ ☐
_____ ☐
_____ ☐
_____ ☐
_____ ☐
_____ ☐
_____ ☐
_____ ☐
_____ ☐
_____ ☐
_____ ☐
_____ ☐

COMMENTS: _____

A Daily Planner

DATE: _____

FAMILY

PERSONAL

THINGS TO DO:

_____ ☐
_____ ☐
_____ ☐
_____ ☐
_____ ☐
_____ ☐
_____ ☐
_____ ☐
_____ ☐
_____ ☐
_____ ☐
_____ ☐
_____ ☐
_____ ☐
_____ ☐
_____ ☐
_____ ☐
_____ ☐
_____ ☐
_____ ☐
_____ ☐

COMMENTS: _____

A Daily Planner

DATE:

FAMILY

THINGS TO DO:

_____ ☐
_____ ☐
_____ ☐
_____ ☐
_____ ☐
_____ ☐
_____ ☐
_____ ☐
_____ ☐
_____ ☐

PERSONAL

_____ ☐
_____ ☐
_____ ☐
_____ ☐
_____ ☐
_____ ☐
_____ ☐
_____ ☐
_____ ☐
_____ ☐

COMMENTS: _____
_____

A Daily Planner

DATE:

FAMILY

PERSONAL

THINGS TO DO:

COMMENTS: _____

A Daily Planner

DATE:

FAMILY

THINGS TO DO:

_____ ☐
_____ ☐
_____ ☐
_____ ☐
_____ ☐
_____ ☐
_____ ☐
_____ ☐
_____ ☐
_____ ☐
_____ ☐
_____ ☐
_____ ☐
_____ ☐
_____ ☐
_____ ☐
_____ ☐
_____ ☐
_____ ☐
_____ ☐
_____ ☐
_____ ☐

PERSONAL

COMMENTS: _____

A Daily Planner

DATE:

FAMILY

THINGS TO DO:

PERSONAL

COMMENTS: _____

A Daily Planner

DATE:

FAMILY

THINGS TO DO:

PERSONAL

COMMENTS: _____

A Daily Planner

DATE:

FAMILY

THINGS TO DO:

PERSONAL

COMMENTS: _____

A Daily Planner

DATE:

FAMILY

THINGS TO DO:

_____ ☐
_____ ☐
_____ ☐
_____ ☐
_____ ☐
_____ ☐
_____ ☐
_____ ☐
_____ ☐
_____ ☐
_____ ☐
_____ ☐
_____ ☐
_____ ☐
_____ ☐
_____ ☐
_____ ☐
_____ ☐
_____ ☐
_____ ☐
_____ ☐

PERSONAL

COMMENTS: _____

_____

A Daily Planner

DATE:

FAMILY

THINGS TO DO:

PERSONAL

COMMENTS: _____

A Daily Planner

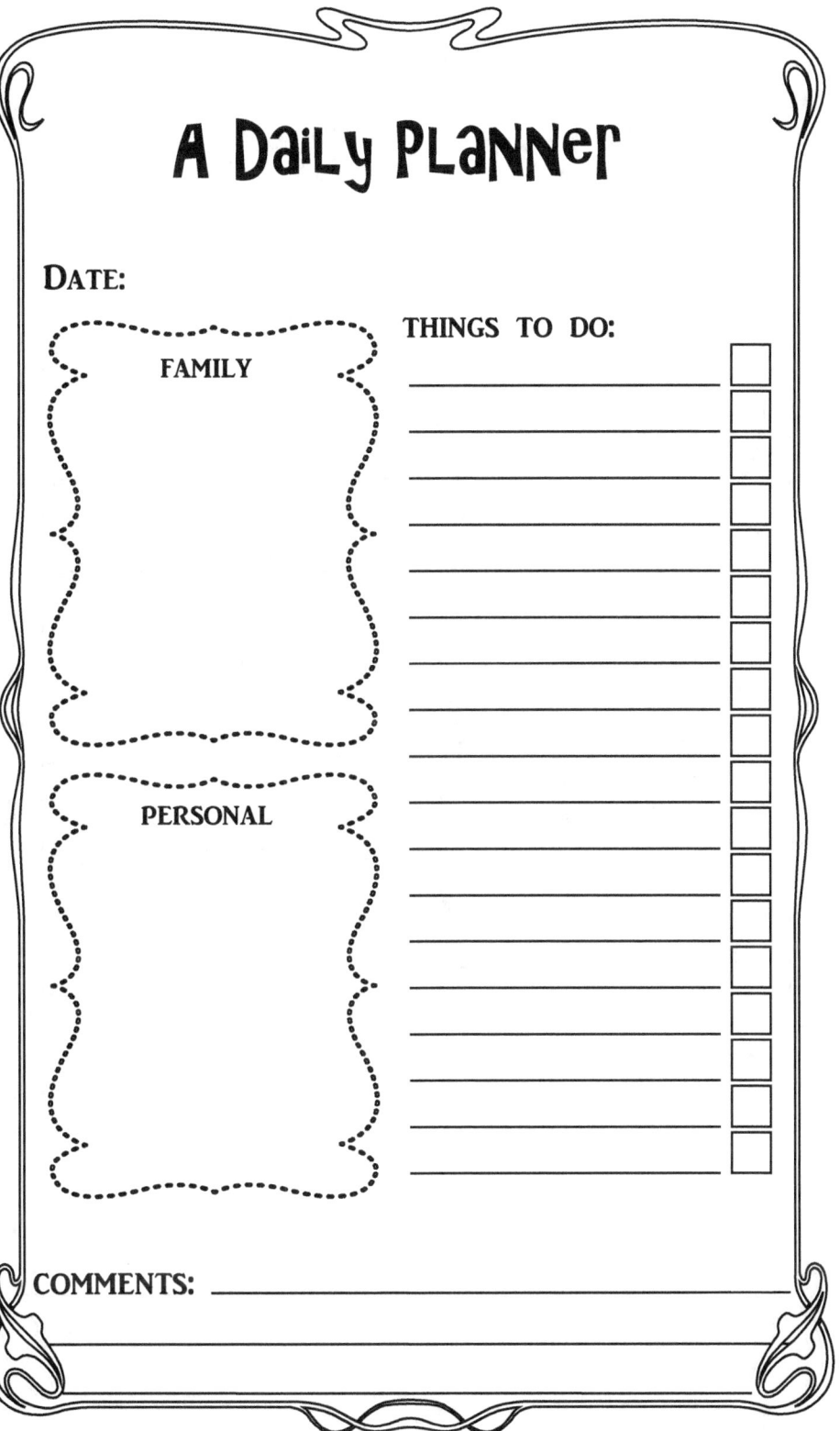

DATE:

FAMILY

PERSONAL

THINGS TO DO:

COMMENTS:

A Daily Planner

DATE:

FAMILY

PERSONAL

THINGS TO DO:

☐
☐
☐
☐
☐
☐
☐
☐
☐
☐
☐
☐
☐
☐
☐
☐
☐
☐
☐
☐

COMMENTS: _____

A Daily Planner

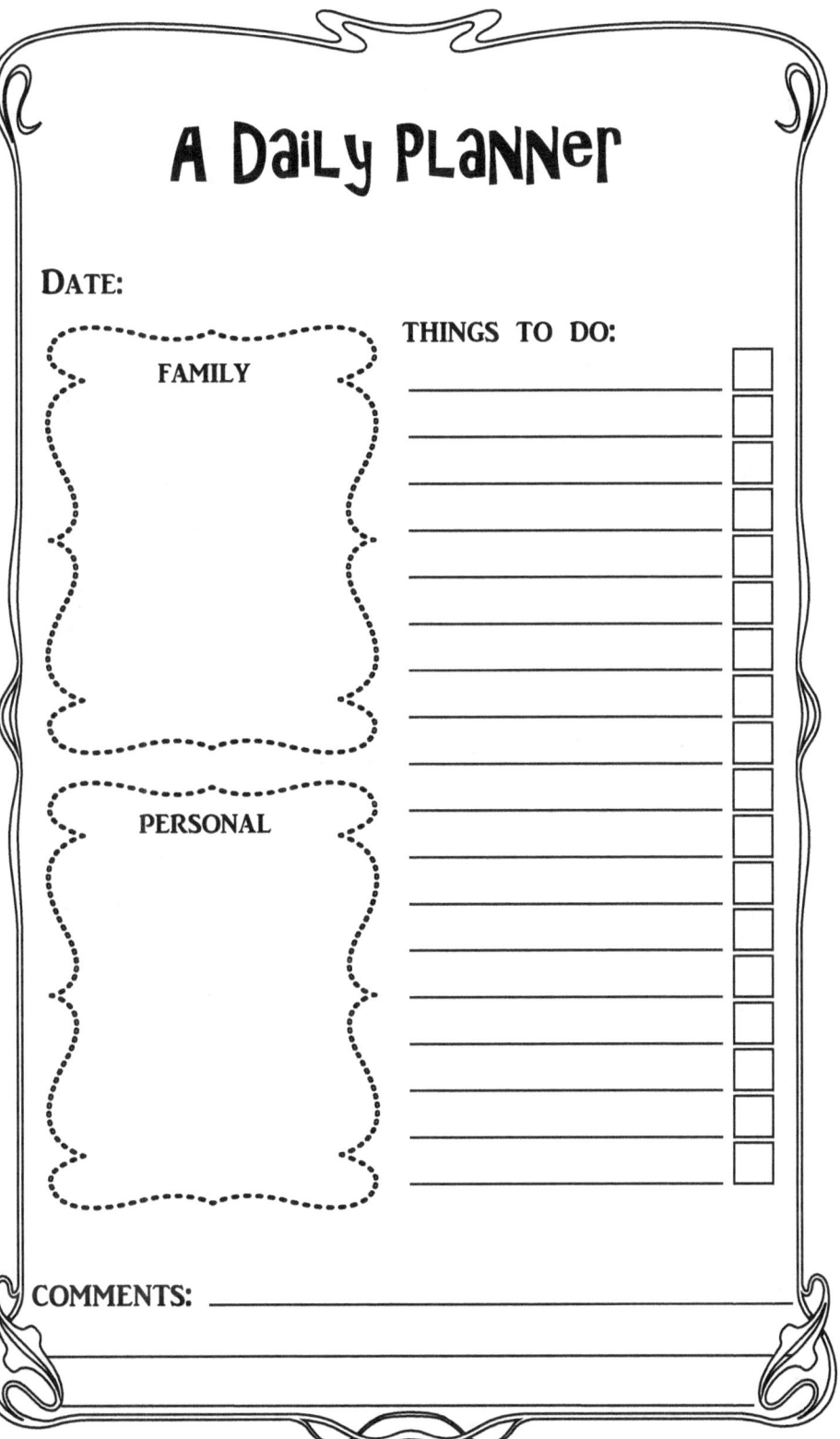

DATE:

FAMILY

PERSONAL

THINGS TO DO:

COMMENTS:

A Daily Planner

DATE:

FAMILY

PERSONAL

THINGS TO DO:

COMMENTS:

A Daily Planner

DATE:

FAMILY

THINGS TO DO:

PERSONAL

COMMENTS: _____

_____

A Daily Planner

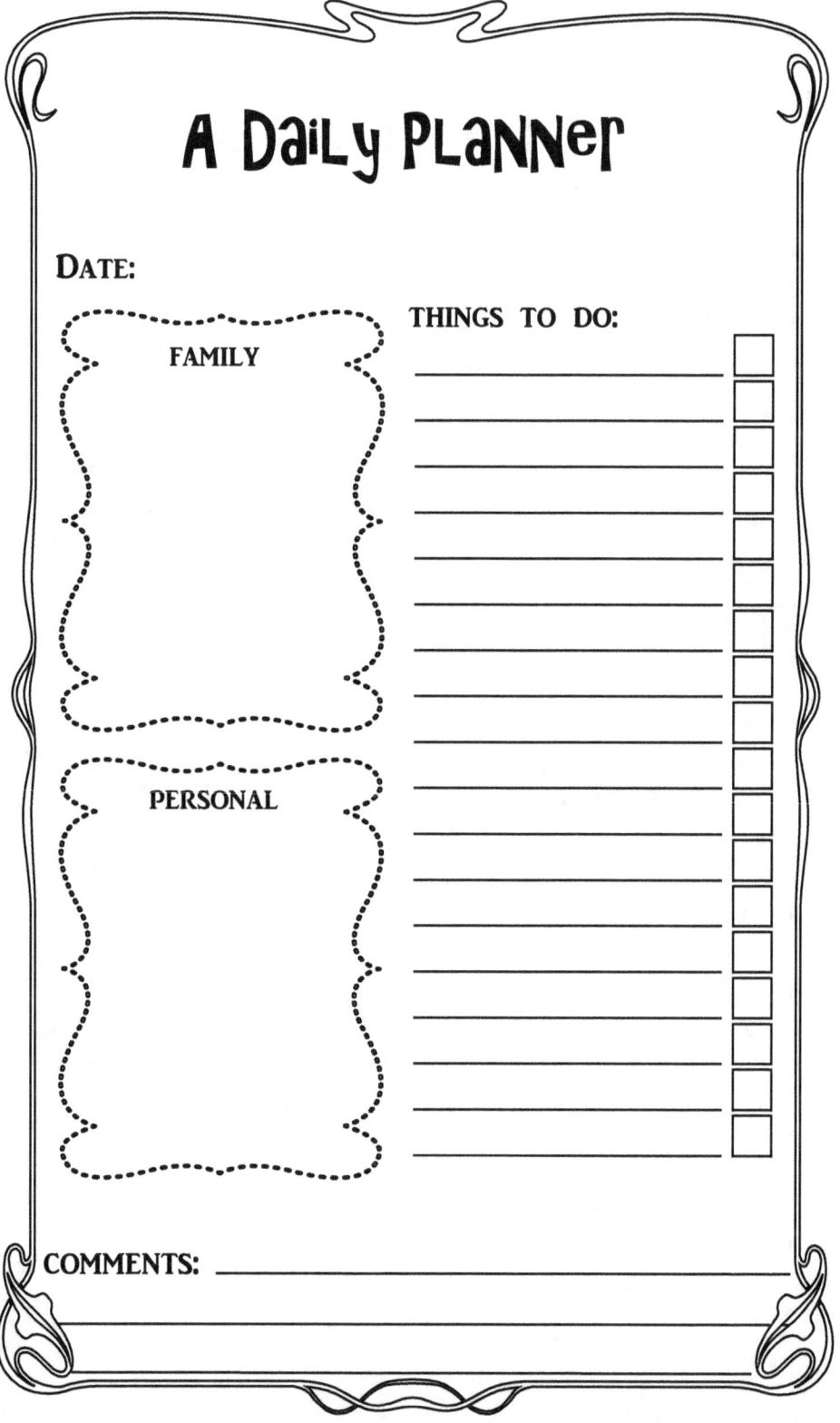

DATE:

FAMILY

PERSONAL

THINGS TO DO:

COMMENTS: _____

A Daily Planner

DATE:

FAMILY

PERSONAL

THINGS TO DO:

COMMENTS:

A Daily Planner

DATE:

FAMILY

PERSONAL

THINGS TO DO:

COMMENTS:

A Daily Planner

DATE:

FAMILY

PERSONAL

THINGS TO DO:

COMMENTS: _____

A Daily Planner

DATE:

FAMILY

THINGS TO DO:

PERSONAL

COMMENTS:

A Daily Planner

DATE:

FAMILY

PERSONAL

THINGS TO DO:

COMMENTS: _____

A Daily Planner

DATE:

FAMILY

PERSONAL

THINGS TO DO:

COMMENTS: _____

A Daily Planner

DATE: _____

FAMILY

PERSONAL

THINGS TO DO:

_____ ☐
_____ ☐
_____ ☐
_____ ☐
_____ ☐
_____ ☐
_____ ☐
_____ ☐
_____ ☐
_____ ☐
_____ ☐
_____ ☐
_____ ☐
_____ ☐
_____ ☐
_____ ☐
_____ ☐
_____ ☐
_____ ☐
_____ ☐

COMMENTS: _____

A Daily Planner

DATE:

FAMILY

THINGS TO DO:

☐
☐
☐
☐
☐
☐
☐
☐
☐
☐
☐
☐
☐
☐
☐
☐
☐
☐
☐
☐
☐

PERSONAL

COMMENTS: _____

A Daily Planner

DATE:

FAMILY

THINGS TO DO:

PERSONAL

COMMENTS: _____

A Daily Planner

DATE:

FAMILY

PERSONAL

THINGS TO DO:

COMMENTS: _____

A Daily Planner

DATE:

FAMILY

THINGS TO DO:

PERSONAL

COMMENTS: _____

A Daily Planner

DATE:

FAMILY

THINGS TO DO:

_____ ☐
_____ ☐
_____ ☐
_____ ☐
_____ ☐
_____ ☐
_____ ☐
_____ ☐
_____ ☐
_____ ☐
_____ ☐

PERSONAL

_____ ☐
_____ ☐
_____ ☐
_____ ☐
_____ ☐
_____ ☐
_____ ☐
_____ ☐
_____ ☐

COMMENTS: _____

A Daily Planner

DATE:

FAMILY

THINGS TO DO:

PERSONAL

COMMENTS: _____

A Daily Planner

DATE:

FAMILY

PERSONAL

THINGS TO DO:

COMMENTS: _____

A Daily Planner

DATE:

FAMILY

THINGS TO DO:

_____ ☐
_____ ☐
_____ ☐
_____ ☐
_____ ☐
_____ ☐
_____ ☐
_____ ☐
_____ ☐
_____ ☐

PERSONAL

_____ ☐
_____ ☐
_____ ☐
_____ ☐
_____ ☐
_____ ☐
_____ ☐
_____ ☐
_____ ☐
_____ ☐
_____ ☐

COMMENTS: _____
_____

A Daily Planner

DATE: _____

FAMILY

THINGS TO DO:

_____ ☐
_____ ☐
_____ ☐
_____ ☐
_____ ☐
_____ ☐
_____ ☐
_____ ☐
_____ ☐
_____ ☐

PERSONAL

_____ ☐
_____ ☐
_____ ☐
_____ ☐
_____ ☐
_____ ☐
_____ ☐
_____ ☐
_____ ☐
_____ ☐

COMMENTS: _____
_____

A Daily Planner

DATE:

FAMILY

THINGS TO DO:

PERSONAL

COMMENTS: _____

A Daily Planner

DATE:

FAMILY

PERSONAL

THINGS TO DO:

COMMENTS: _____

A Daily Planner

DATE:

FAMILY

PERSONAL

THINGS TO DO:

COMMENTS: _____

A Daily Planner

DATE:

FAMILY

THINGS TO DO:

PERSONAL

COMMENTS: _____

A Daily Planner

DATE:

FAMILY

THINGS TO DO:

☐
☐
☐
☐
☐
☐
☐
☐
☐
☐
☐
☐
☐
☐
☐
☐
☐
☐
☐
☐
☐
☐

PERSONAL

COMMENTS: _____

A Daily Planner

DATE:

FAMILY

THINGS TO DO:

PERSONAL

COMMENTS:

A Daily Planner

DATE:

FAMILY

PERSONAL

THINGS TO DO:

COMMENTS: _____

A Daily Planner

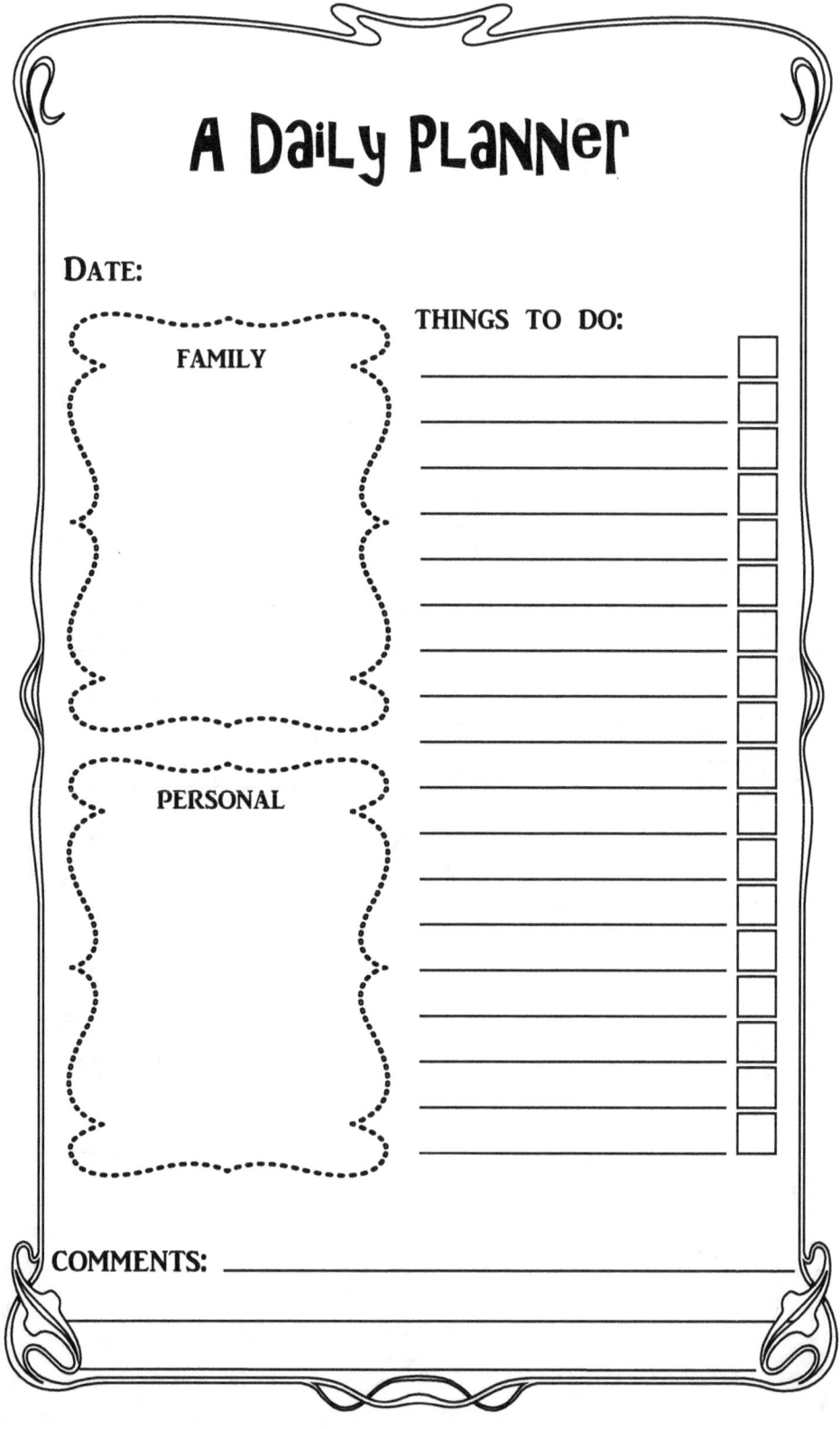

DATE:

FAMILY

PERSONAL

THINGS TO DO:

COMMENTS:

A Daily Planner

DATE:

FAMILY

THINGS TO DO:

PERSONAL

COMMENTS: _____

A Daily Planner

DATE:

FAMILY

PERSONAL

THINGS TO DO:

COMMENTS:

A Daily Planner

DATE:

FAMILY

PERSONAL

THINGS TO DO:

COMMENTS: _____

A Daily Planner

DATE:

FAMILY

THINGS TO DO:

PERSONAL

COMMENTS: _____

A Daily Planner

DATE:

FAMILY

PERSONAL

THINGS TO DO:

_____ ☐
_____ ☐
_____ ☐
_____ ☐
_____ ☐
_____ ☐
_____ ☐
_____ ☐
_____ ☐
_____ ☐
_____ ☐
_____ ☐
_____ ☐
_____ ☐
_____ ☐
_____ ☐
_____ ☐
_____ ☐
_____ ☐
_____ ☐
_____ ☐
_____ ☐

COMMENTS: _____

A Daily Planner

DATE:

FAMILY

PERSONAL

THINGS TO DO:

COMMENTS: _____

A Daily Planner

DATE:

FAMILY

PERSONAL

THINGS TO DO:

COMMENTS: _____

A Daily Planner

DATE:

FAMILY

THINGS TO DO:

PERSONAL

COMMENTS: _____

A Daily Planner

DATE:

FAMILY

PERSONAL

THINGS TO DO:

☐
☐
☐
☐
☐
☐
☐
☐
☐
☐
☐
☐
☐
☐
☐
☐
☐
☐
☐
☐
☐

COMMENTS: _____

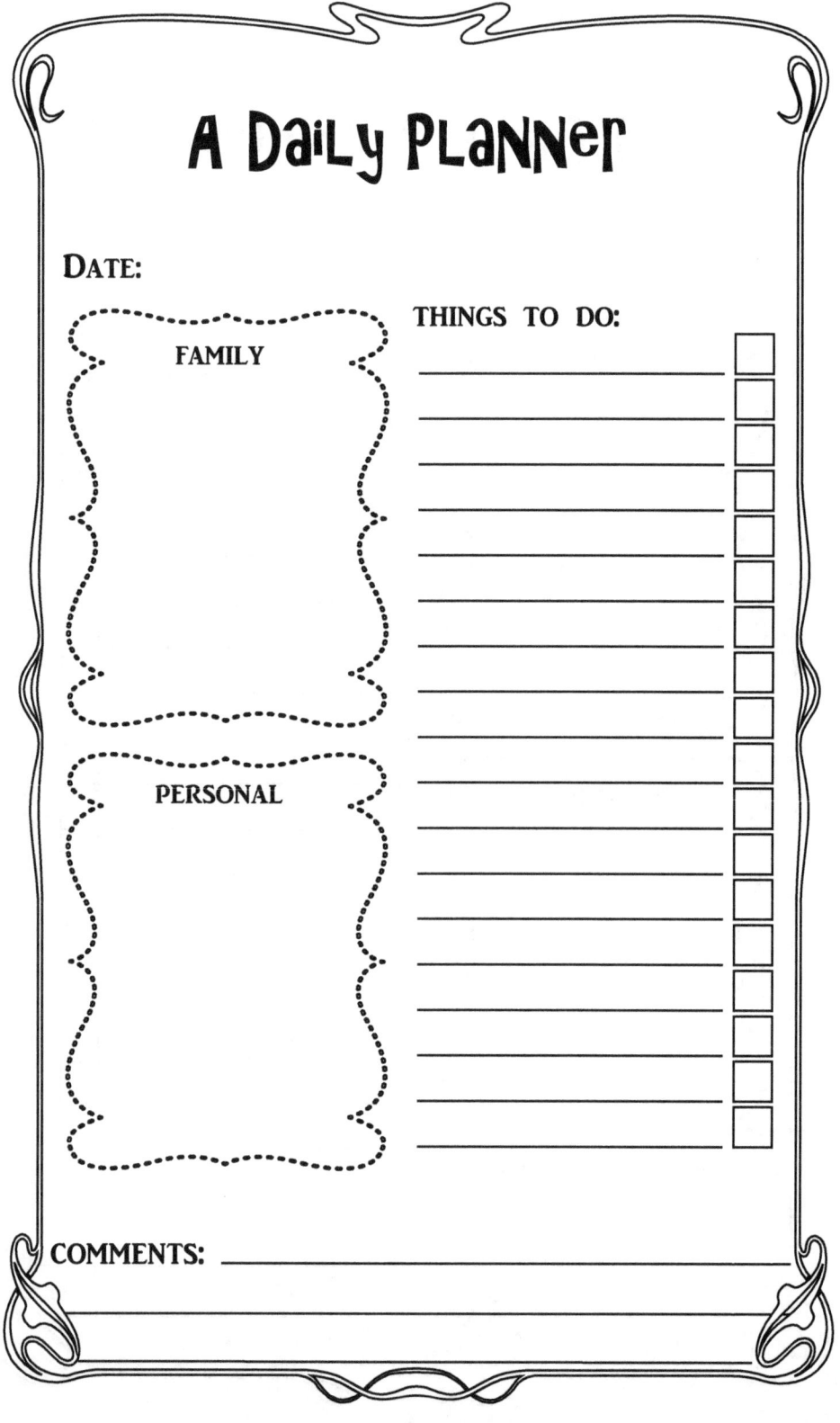

A Daily Planner

DATE:

FAMILY

THINGS TO DO:

PERSONAL

COMMENTS: _____

A Daily Planner

DATE:

FAMILY

THINGS TO DO:

PERSONAL

COMMENTS: _____

A Daily Planner

DATE:

FAMILY

THINGS TO DO:

_____ ☐
_____ ☐
_____ ☐
_____ ☐
_____ ☐
_____ ☐
_____ ☐
_____ ☐
_____ ☐
_____ ☐
_____ ☐
_____ ☐
_____ ☐
_____ ☐
_____ ☐
_____ ☐
_____ ☐
_____ ☐
_____ ☐
_____ ☐

PERSONAL

COMMENTS: _____
_____

A Daily Planner

DATE:

FAMILY

PERSONAL

THINGS TO DO:
_____ ☐
_____ ☐
_____ ☐
_____ ☐
_____ ☐
_____ ☐
_____ ☐
_____ ☐
_____ ☐
_____ ☐
_____ ☐
_____ ☐
_____ ☐
_____ ☐
_____ ☐
_____ ☐
_____ ☐
_____ ☐
_____ ☐
_____ ☐

COMMENTS: _____

A Daily Planner

DATE:

FAMILY

THINGS TO DO:

PERSONAL

COMMENTS: _____

A Daily Planner

DATE:

FAMILY

PERSONAL

THINGS TO DO:

COMMENTS: _____

A Daily Planner

DATE:

FAMILY

PERSONAL

THINGS TO DO:

COMMENTS: _____

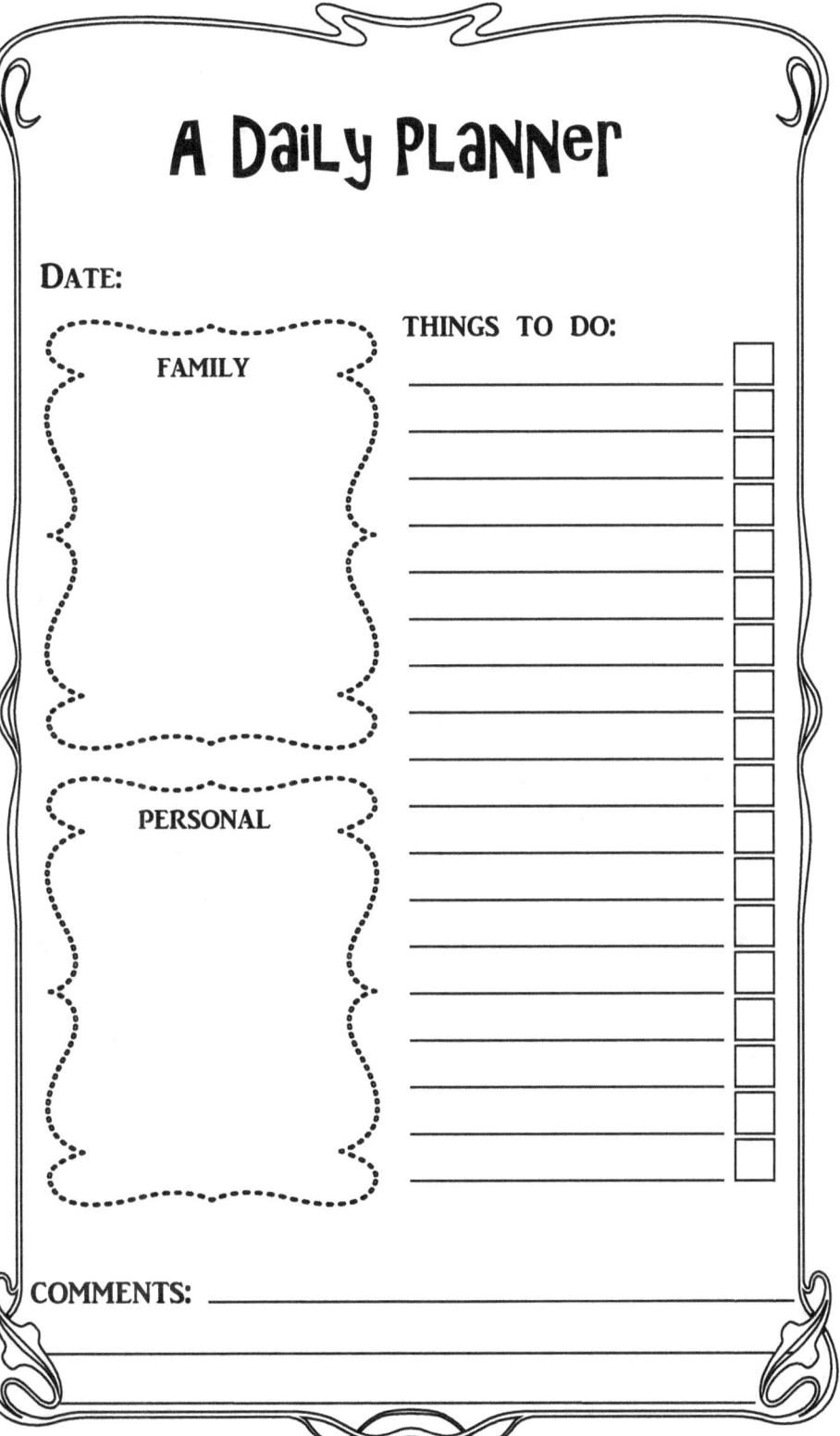

A Daily Planner

DATE:

FAMILY

PERSONAL

THINGS TO DO:

COMMENTS: _____

A Daily Planner

DATE:

FAMILY

THINGS TO DO:

PERSONAL

COMMENTS: _____

A Daily Planner

DATE:

FAMILY

THINGS TO DO:

PERSONAL

COMMENTS: _____

A Daily Planner

DATE:

FAMILY

PERSONAL

THINGS TO DO:

COMMENTS: _____

A Daily Planner

DATE:

FAMILY

PERSONAL

THINGS TO DO:

COMMENTS: _____

A Daily Planner

DATE:

FAMILY

THINGS TO DO:

_____ ☐
_____ ☐
_____ ☐
_____ ☐
_____ ☐
_____ ☐
_____ ☐
_____ ☐
_____ ☐
_____ ☐
_____ ☐

PERSONAL

_____ ☐
_____ ☐
_____ ☐
_____ ☐
_____ ☐
_____ ☐
_____ ☐
_____ ☐
_____ ☐

COMMENTS: _____

A Daily Planner

DATE:

FAMILY

PERSONAL

THINGS TO DO:

COMMENTS: _____

A Daily Planner

DATE:

FAMILY

PERSONAL

THINGS TO DO:

COMMENTS: _____

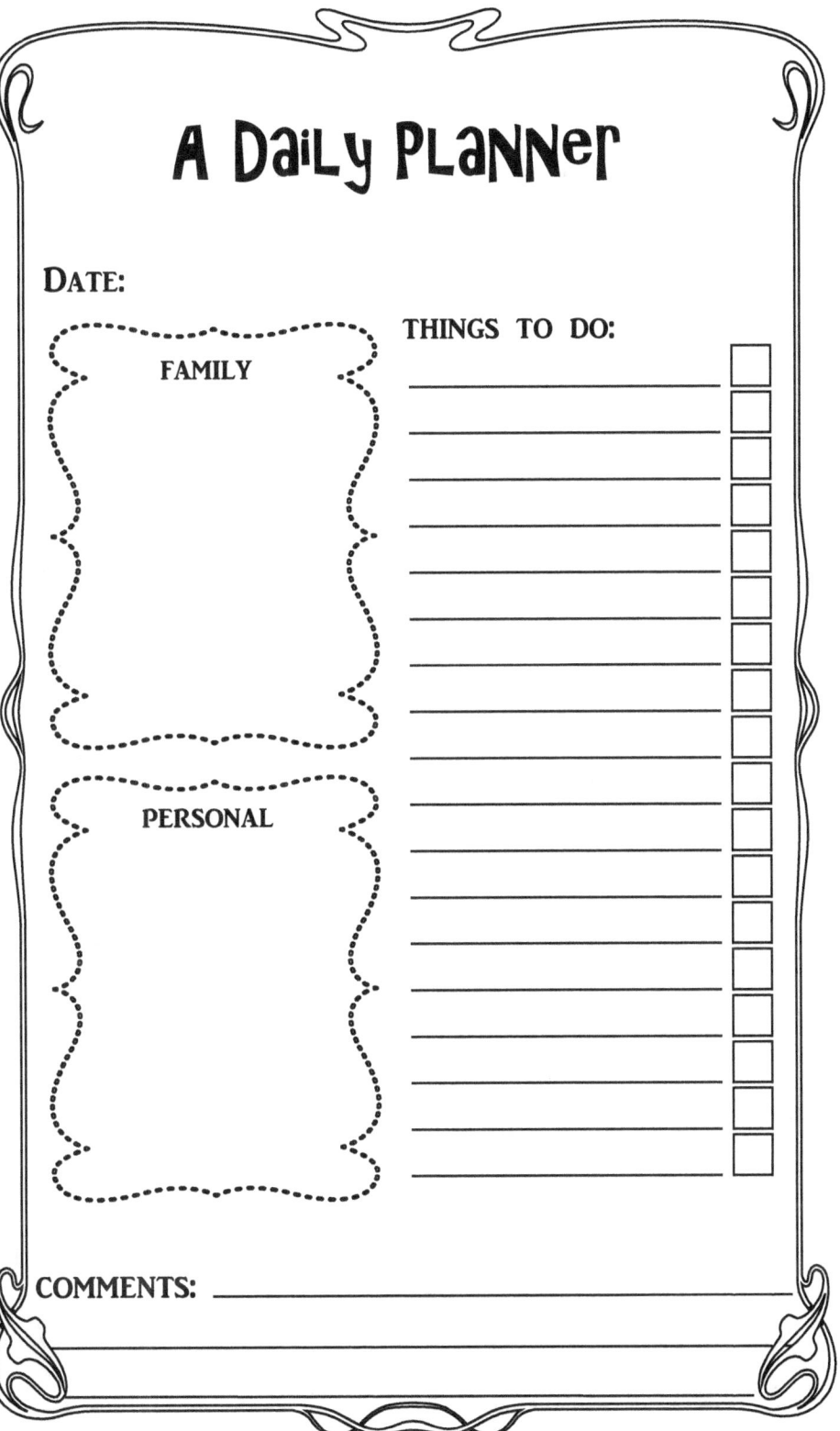

A Daily Planner

DATE:

FAMILY

PERSONAL

THINGS TO DO:

COMMENTS:

A Daily Planner

DATE:

FAMILY

THINGS TO DO:

PERSONAL

COMMENTS: _____

A Daily Planner

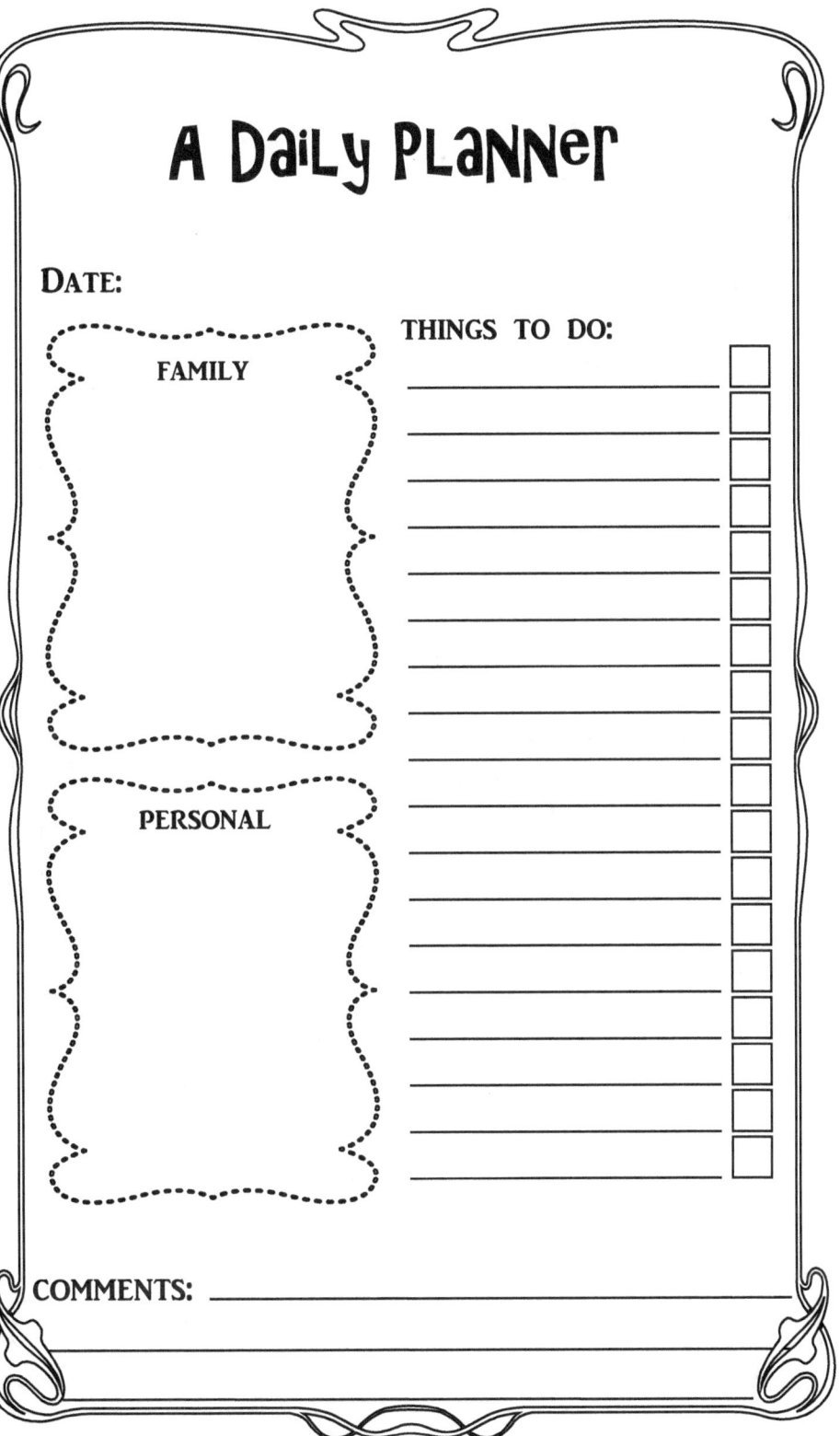

DATE:

FAMILY

PERSONAL

THINGS TO DO:

COMMENTS: _____

A Daily Planner

DATE:

FAMILY

PERSONAL

THINGS TO DO:

COMMENTS: _____

A Daily Planner

DATE:

FAMILY

PERSONAL

THINGS TO DO:

COMMENTS: _____

A Daily Planner

DATE:

FAMILY

THINGS TO DO:

PERSONAL

COMMENTS: _____

A Daily Planner

DATE:

FAMILY

PERSONAL

THINGS TO DO:

COMMENTS:

A Daily Planner

DATE:

FAMILY

THINGS TO DO:

PERSONAL

COMMENTS: _____

A Daily Planner

DATE:

FAMILY

THINGS TO DO:

PERSONAL

COMMENTS:

A Daily Planner

DATE:

FAMILY

PERSONAL

THINGS TO DO:

COMMENTS:

A Daily Planner

DATE:

FAMILY

THINGS TO DO:

PERSONAL

COMMENTS: _____

A Daily Planner

DATE:

FAMILY

PERSONAL

THINGS TO DO:

_____ ☐
_____ ☐
_____ ☐
_____ ☐
_____ ☐
_____ ☐
_____ ☐
_____ ☐
_____ ☐
_____ ☐
_____ ☐
_____ ☐
_____ ☐
_____ ☐
_____ ☐
_____ ☐
_____ ☐
_____ ☐
_____ ☐
_____ ☐

COMMENTS: _____

A Daily Planner

DATE:

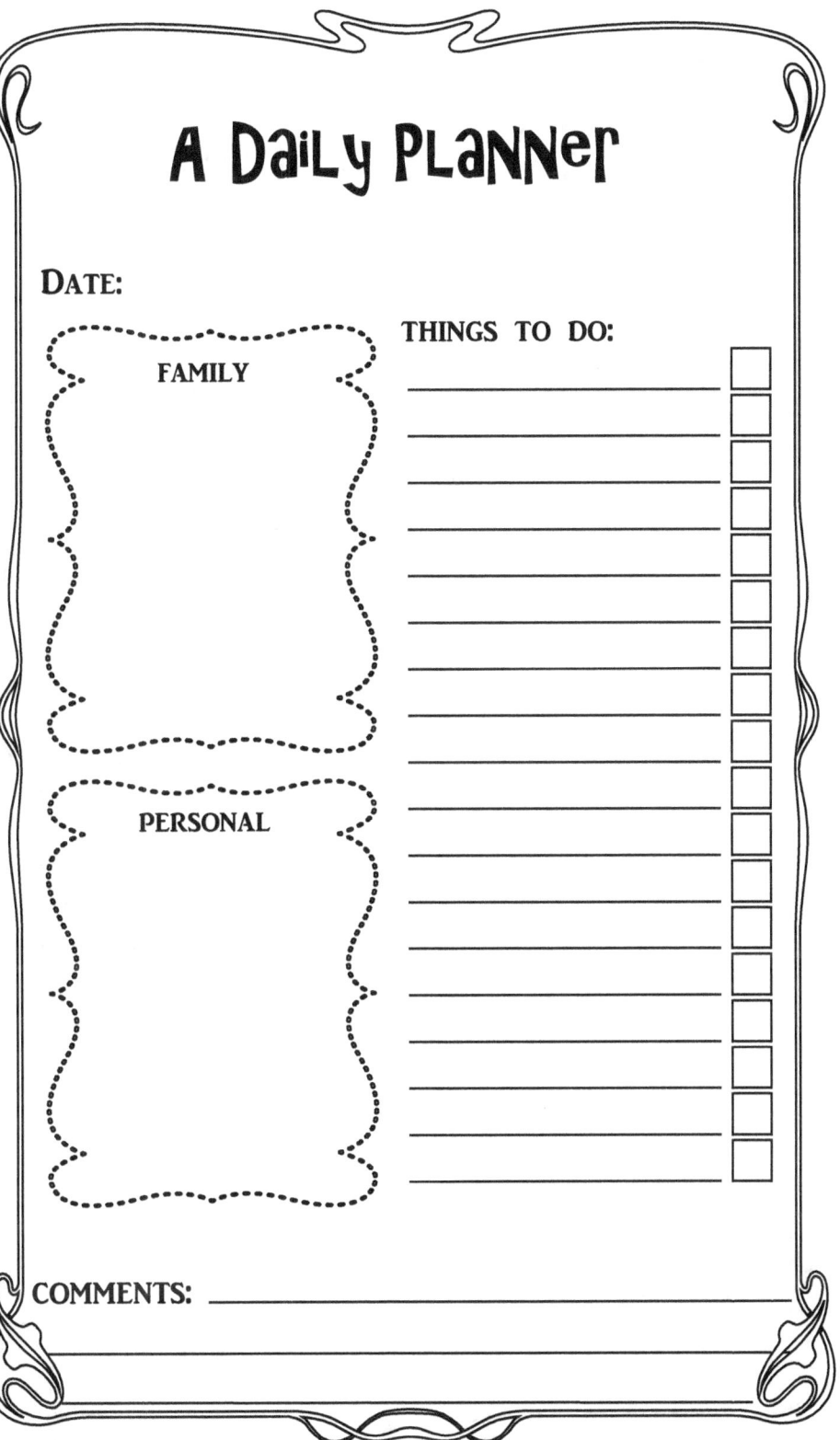

FAMILY

PERSONAL

THINGS TO DO:

☐
☐
☐
☐
☐
☐
☐
☐
☐
☐
☐
☐
☐
☐
☐
☐
☐
☐
☐
☐
☐

COMMENTS: _____

A Daily Planner

DATE:

FAMILY

THINGS TO DO:

PERSONAL

COMMENTS:

A Daily Planner

DATE:

FAMILY

THINGS TO DO:

_____ □
_____ □
_____ □
_____ □
_____ □
_____ □
_____ □
_____ □
_____ □
_____ □
_____ □
_____ □

PERSONAL

_____ □
_____ □
_____ □
_____ □
_____ □
_____ □
_____ □
_____ □
_____ □

COMMENTS: _____

A Daily Planner

DATE:

FAMILY

PERSONAL

THINGS TO DO:

_____

_____

_____

_____

_____

_____

_____

_____

_____

_____

_____

_____

_____

_____

_____

_____

_____

_____

_____

COMMENTS: _____

A Daily Planner

DATE:

FAMILY

PERSONAL

THINGS TO DO:

COMMENTS:

A Daily Planner

DATE:

FAMILY

THINGS TO DO:

PERSONAL

COMMENTS: _____

A Daily Planner

DATE:

FAMILY

THINGS TO DO:

PERSONAL

COMMENTS: _____

A Daily Planner

DATE:

FAMILY

THINGS TO DO:

PERSONAL

COMMENTS: _____

A Daily Planner

DATE:

FAMILY

PERSONAL

THINGS TO DO:

_____ ☐
_____ ☐
_____ ☐
_____ ☐
_____ ☐
_____ ☐
_____ ☐
_____ ☐
_____ ☐
_____ ☐
_____ ☐
_____ ☐
_____ ☐
_____ ☐
_____ ☐
_____ ☐
_____ ☐
_____ ☐
_____ ☐
_____ ☐
_____ ☐

COMMENTS: _____

A Daily Planner

DATE:

FAMILY

PERSONAL

THINGS TO DO:

COMMENTS: _____

A Daily Planner

DATE:

FAMILY

THINGS TO DO:

PERSONAL

COMMENTS: _____

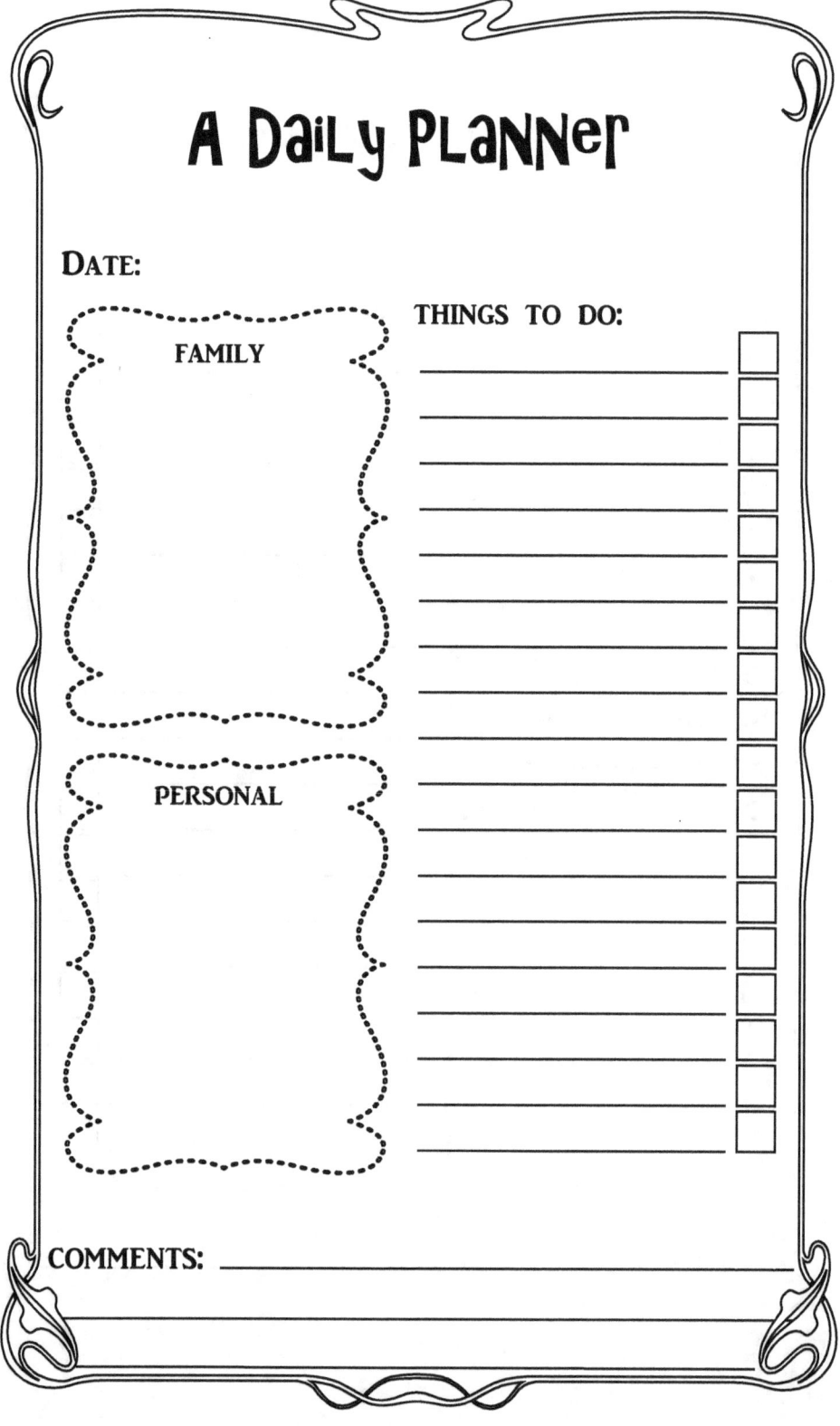

A Daily Planner

DATE:

FAMILY

PERSONAL

THINGS TO DO:

COMMENTS: _____

A Daily Planner

DATE:

FAMILY

PERSONAL

THINGS TO DO:

_____ ☐
_____ ☐
_____ ☐
_____ ☐
_____ ☐
_____ ☐
_____ ☐
_____ ☐
_____ ☐
_____ ☐
_____ ☐
_____ ☐
_____ ☐
_____ ☐
_____ ☐
_____ ☐
_____ ☐
_____ ☐
_____ ☐
_____ ☐
_____ ☐
_____ ☐

COMMENTS: _____

A Daily Planner

DATE:

FAMILY

PERSONAL

THINGS TO DO:

COMMENTS:

A Daily Planner

DATE: _____

FAMILY

PERSONAL

THINGS TO DO:

COMMENTS: _____

A Daily Planner

DATE:

FAMILY

THINGS TO DO:

PERSONAL

COMMENTS: _____

A Daily Planner

DATE:

FAMILY

THINGS TO DO:

_____
_____
_____
_____
_____
_____
_____
_____
_____
_____
_____

PERSONAL

_____
_____
_____
_____
_____
_____
_____
_____
_____
_____
_____

COMMENTS: _____

A Daily Planner

DATE:

FAMILY

PERSONAL

THINGS TO DO:

COMMENTS:

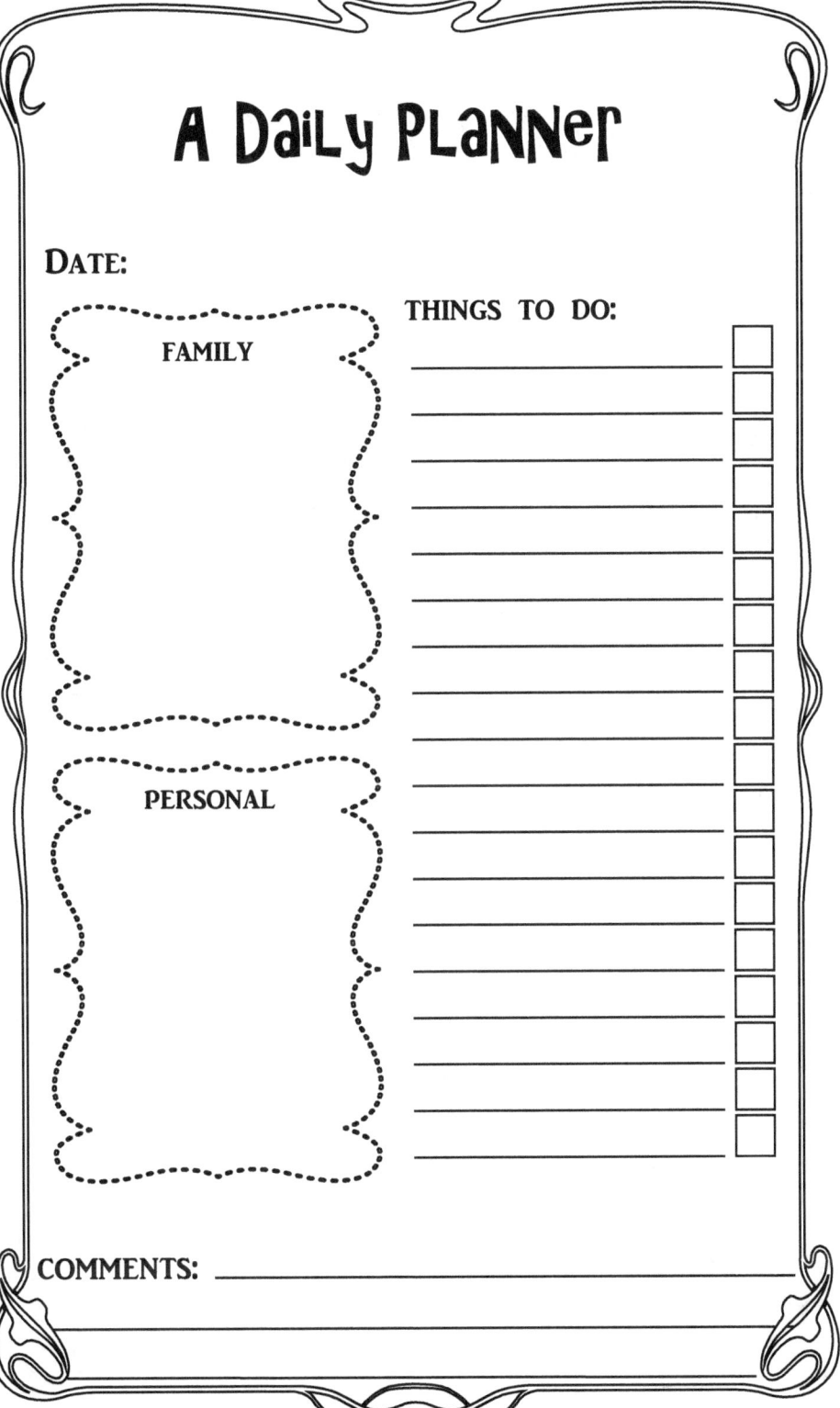

A Daily Planner

DATE:

FAMILY

PERSONAL

THINGS TO DO:

COMMENTS:

A Daily Planner

DATE:

FAMILY

THINGS TO DO:

_____ ☐
_____ ☐
_____ ☐
_____ ☐
_____ ☐
_____ ☐
_____ ☐
_____ ☐
_____ ☐
_____ ☐
_____ ☐
_____ ☐
_____ ☐

PERSONAL

_____ ☐
_____ ☐
_____ ☐
_____ ☐
_____ ☐
_____ ☐
_____ ☐
_____ ☐
_____ ☐
_____ ☐

COMMENTS: _____

A Daily Planner

DATE:

FAMILY

PERSONAL

THINGS TO DO:

COMMENTS: _____

A Daily Planner

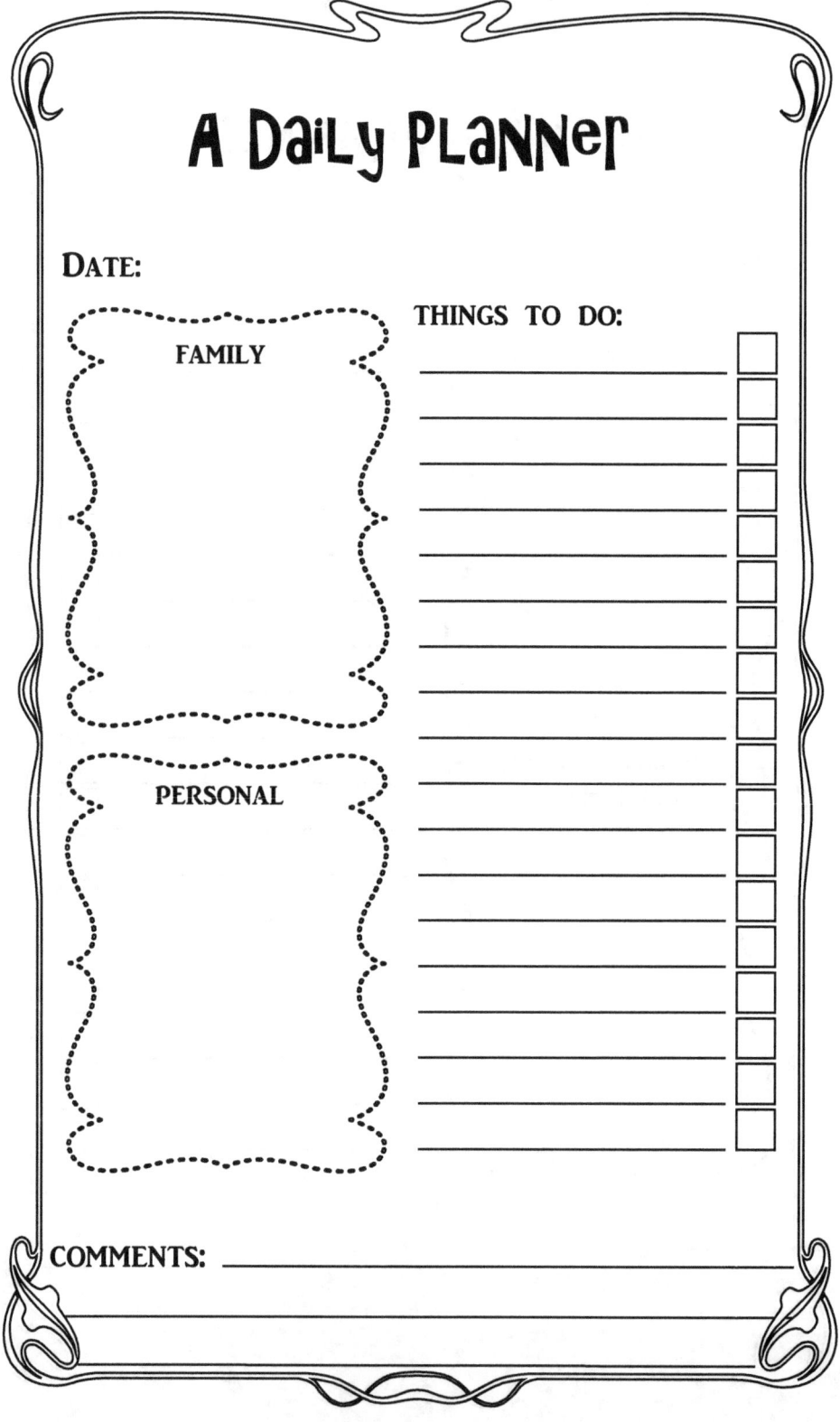

DATE:

FAMILY

PERSONAL

THINGS TO DO:

COMMENTS:

A Daily Planner

DATE:

FAMILY

THINGS TO DO:

PERSONAL

COMMENTS: _____

A Daily Planner

DATE:

FAMILY

PERSONAL

THINGS TO DO:

COMMENTS: _____

A Daily Planner

DATE:

FAMILY

PERSONAL

THINGS TO DO:

☐
☐
☐
☐
☐
☐
☐
☐
☐
☐
☐
☐
☐
☐
☐
☐
☐
☐
☐

COMMENTS:

A Daily Planner

DATE: _____

FAMILY

THINGS TO DO:

_____ ☐
_____ ☐
_____ ☐
_____ ☐
_____ ☐
_____ ☐
_____ ☐
_____ ☐

PERSONAL

_____ ☐
_____ ☐
_____ ☐
_____ ☐
_____ ☐
_____ ☐
_____ ☐
_____ ☐
_____ ☐
_____ ☐
_____ ☐
_____ ☐

COMMENTS: _____
_____

A Daily Planner

DATE:

FAMILY

PERSONAL

THINGS TO DO:

_____ ☐
_____ ☐
_____ ☐
_____ ☐
_____ ☐
_____ ☐
_____ ☐
_____ ☐
_____ ☐
_____ ☐
_____ ☐
_____ ☐
_____ ☐
_____ ☐
_____ ☐
_____ ☐
_____ ☐
_____ ☐
_____ ☐
_____ ☐
_____ ☐

COMMENTS: _____
_____

www.ingramcontent.com/pod-product-compliance
Lightning Source LLC
Chambersburg PA
CBHW080736250626
47170CB00010B/2852